AF214889

marias-magische-manuskripte.de

© 2022 Maria Thiele

Illustrated by: **Maria Thiele &
Emily Thiele** (poster classroom)
Translated by: **Jennifer Crutchfield**
Photographs by: **Eve Pliewischkies**
Correction by: **Sigrid Wagner**

Language of original edition: German
Publisher label: Maria´s magische Manuskripte

ISBN Softcover: 978-3-347-88250-8
ISBN Hardcover: 978-3-347-88660-5
ISBN E-Book: 978-3-347-88251-5

Printing and distribution on behalf of the author:
tredition GmbH, Halenreie 40-44, 22359 Hamburg, Germany

My Stepmom is a Witch

For Emily & Johannes

You are magical!

Hello, my name is Taylor. And this here next to me is Simba, our family cat.

One morning we just found him lounging around in front of our door. Eliza said that he had chosen us to be his family. So we decided to let him stay.

Except for his unusual name, he's just a normal cuddly black cat. Just as normal as I am.

Would you like to know what I do all day?

I love roaming around outside or burying my nose in books filled with fantastical and magical worlds.

On the weekends, my parents and I enjoy playing board games for hours.

These are my parents.

My dad Alexander can be pretty silly and is always up to some kind of nonsense. He is also a great baker and I love making cookies with him – which we always end up devouring in our pillow fort.

Eliza is the one who builds the pillow forts. She is my stepmom and a real bundle of energy.

She helps me clean up super-fast, so that we always end up having enough time to play a video game or craft something out of the many treasures I collect in my jacket pockets.

Oh wait; don't you know what a stepmom is?

Well, Eliza always calls me her bonus-child and I prefer to call her my bonus-mom instead of my stepmom.

A stepmom lives together with your mom or dad and takes care of you. She helps with homework, takes you on trips, and may sometimes even scold you – just like any regular mom. The difference is that she didn't give birth to you.

Some people have a mom and a bonus-mom because their mom and dad didn't get along anymore. Or they may have a bonus-dad together with their dad instead of a bonus-mom.

In my case, my mom is no longer with us – which is why we have Eliza.

By now you already know a lot about me. I do have one more thing to tell you. Can you keep a secret? It's a really big secret.

Eliza is not your average bonus-mom.

She's not even your average woman.

She is a witch.

I SWEAR!

Stop grinning, I have proof – I'll show you.

A while ago I had a really horrible nightmare.

I can't remember exactly what I was dreaming about, but I woke up feeling very scared and couldn't calm myself down. I was worried that the nightmare would continue as soon as I fell asleep again.

So I called out for Mom and Dad.

Eliza came into my room. Immediately, my room felt a lot brighter and more calm.

She came to me and asked how she could help. Then she took me in her arms, patted my back, looked at me, winked and wiggled her nose. Suddenly, I had to yawn and my fears were all gone.

She had just made it all disappear!

And then there's the case of my vocabulary test.

A while back, I had to study for my German Exam.

It felt like a ton of vocabulary to learn, and the more I learned, the more my head was buzzing. Nothing made sense anymore.

At one point, everything was such a mess that I threw my index cards aside in frustration. That's when Dad called me to dinner.

I poked around in my food until Eliza asked me what was going on.

When I told her about my vocabulary chaos, she offered to help me study.

When we had cleared the table, she made us hot chocolates and looked at all the index cards with me.

She took the cards with objects written on them and started placing them on the corresponding items around the house.

We walked around the house together and said the words out loud. That helped a lot.

Eliza also taught me mnemonic devices and thought up stories to help me remember certain words better.

While tucking me in at night, she looked at me, winked and wiggled her nose. And, suddenly, she had brought order to the chaos in my head.

Didn't I tell you? WITCH!

The next day I still had a bit of a queasy feeling during the test, but I was able to remember all of the vocabulary we had learned together.

I finished my test and turned it in with a smile.

When we got the tests back, I was super happy: I had gotten a B!

"I passed!" the voice in my head cheered.

The teacher asked the class how we had studied and whether we had any questions or advice for our classmates.

"Taylor, how did you do it?" She asked me. I took a deep breath and finally decided to give an honest answer.

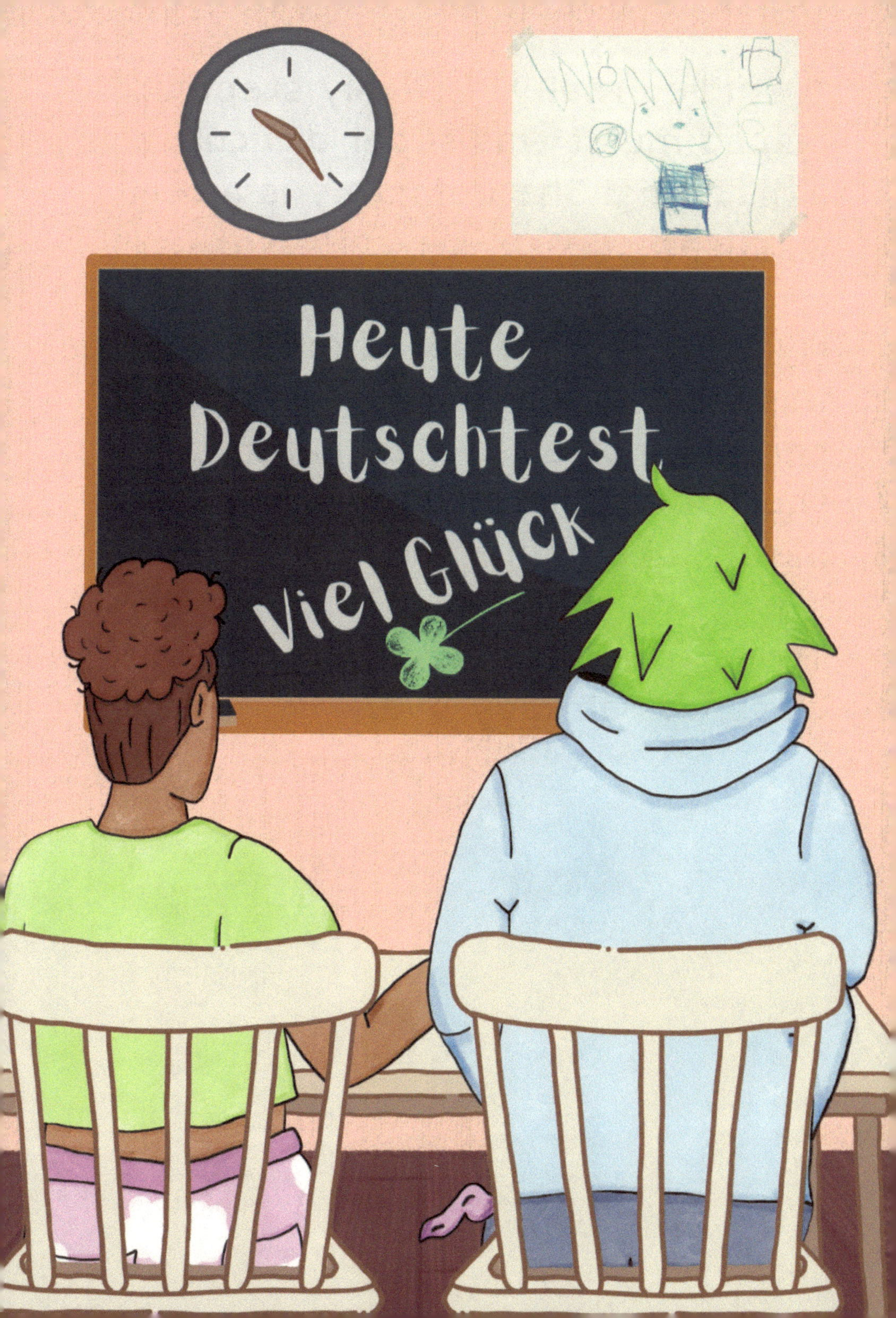
Heute
Deutschtest
Viel Glück

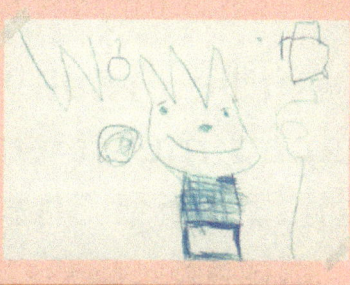

"I studied really hard. My stepmom helped me. It was super difficult and exhausting! She definitely is a real witch. "

My teacher interrupted me to say that this was no way to talk about one's parents, not even step-parents. Then she wrote a note to my parents for me to take home.

I tried to explain what I had meant, but class was already over.

Wow, I guess stepmoms and witches both have a pretty bad reputation.

I didn't mean what I had said in a bad way.

It's just that Eliza is enchanting and brings magic into our lives.

She uses her magic to help us out (and maybe sometimes to play tricks on us).

I must admit that I have never asked her directly if she is a witch.

I just know that it's true.

She has even taught me a magical spell.

Do you know the feeling, when something REALLY annoys you, like when you get angry with your friends?

When you get all hot inside and it feels like you are about to explode...

That's when you have to try and keep calm. Eliza's spell can help you with that.

Here, I'll teach it to you.

Take a deep breath. Close your eyes and start counting:

1-2-3-4-5

When you've reached 5, ask yourself: The thing I'm annoyed about - will it still be important in 5 minutes, 5 hours, 5 days, 5 months and 5 years?

By then your anger will have subsided, because only very few things are really still going to be important in 5 years. And thus – POOF! – your anger has disappeared!

MAGIC!

It's not worth holding in annoyance and anger, that'll just take up the good space inside of you which should better be occupied by feelings of joy and happiness.

Well, there you go.

I told you, my bonus-mom is a witch.

Maybe someone in your family is a witch, too?!

Your mom, or grandma, or your big brother...

Everything is possible!

Hello, my name is Maria and you are holding my first book in your hands.

In 2020, after a long bedtime-story with my daughter, Taylor visited me in my dreams and made me fall in love with the idea of writing a book.

Although our family was going through some stressful times (as I am sure many other families experienced in 2020 as well), Taylor turned out to be a wonderfully welcome break during those hard times.

I myself have a couple of bonus-parents, as I grew up in a loving adoptive family. Now I am married and have become a mom as well.

Taylor helped me to start drawing and also to pursue many of my other ideas and passions.

I hope this is only the first of many more books that I will be able to write and that will captivate you as a reader.

Let yourself be enchanted!

marias-magische-manuskripte.de

You can find even more **magical products** and **enchanting free offers** for young and old on my homepage.

Zeitfracht Medien GmbH
Ferdinand-Jühlke-Straße 7
99095 Erfurt, Deutschland
produktsicherheit@kolibri360.de